TIME TO SHINE

Celebrating the World's
Iridescent Animals

Text by Karen Jameson

Art by Dave Murray

Groundwood Books / House of Anansi Press
Toronto / Berkeley

Each iridescent creature knows
just how to rock its sparkly "clothes."
To draw attention, speed away
or just survive another day.

Iridescence is the rainbow-like shimmer seen on
some bird feathers, fish scales, insect bodies and
more. The brightness and colors of these animals
change, depending on the angle from which
they're seen.

When Morpho butterflies fold up their wings, their brown undersides camouflage with the forest floor. Morphos startle predators with a flash of electric-blue wings to make a quick getaway.

Butterflies make quick escapes
in brilliant iridescent capes.

Male hummingbirds use their ultraviolet colors, along with flying stunts and songs, to dazzle females. They also puff up their feathers in warning as they dive-bomb intruders and guard their territory.

A sequined costume works just great
to land the hummingbird a mate.

Glint, glitter, gleam! Light bouncing off metallic beetles scatters in multiple directions at once, confusing predators hoping to pounce on a tasty meal. This use of iridescence is called dynamic disruptive camouflage.

When their jackets flicker-flash,
beetles *seem* to dart and dash!

A regal peacock loves to reign
by fanning out his feathered train.

To impress females, peacocks pose in the
best light to display the iridescent eyespots
on their feathers. As a defense, the males
make their shimmering tail feathers as big
as they can to frighten off other animals.

Reed frog takes some time to rest
in its sun-reflecting vest.

In dry season, the reed frog's
iridescent skin reflects the sun
to keep its body cooled to the
right temperature. That's called
thermoregulation.

The rainbow boa's iridescence serves as camouflage in the colorful rainforest. Its tightly packed iridescent scales repel water to keep it dry and reduce friction, allowing it to glide smoothly through tight spaces.

Smooth and dry in shiny armor,
rainbow boa's quite the charmer.

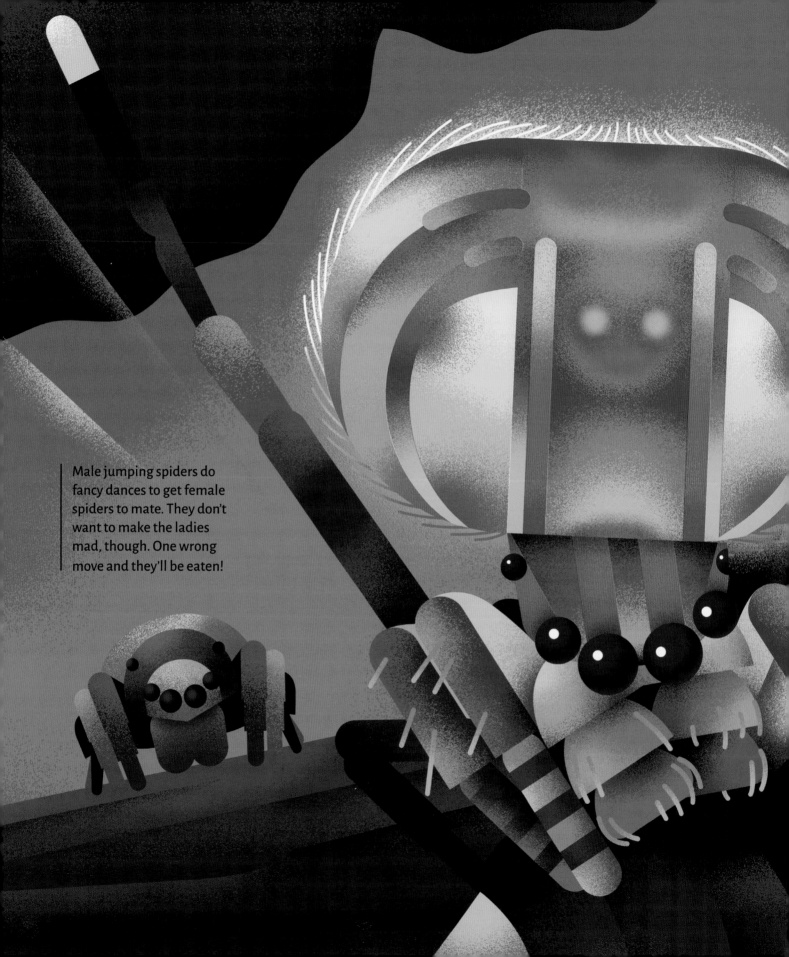

Male jumping spiders do fancy dances to get female spiders to mate. They don't want to make the ladies mad, though. One wrong move and they'll be eaten!

In leggings, jumping spider prances,
showing off his courtship dances.

With striking colors on their wings, dragonflies dart and hover to advertise for mates and claim their territory. They may even point out good spots for the female to lay her eggs.

With flashy sleeves, swift dragonflies zoom around to advertise.

Flocks of mallard ducks use their brightly colored heads and wings as signals to coordinate flight movements and the direction of travel. Glossy green head feathers distinguish the male, while the female's head feathers are a drab brown.

Mallards sporting flying caps
leave behind their travel maps.

Schools of silvery fish join forces to stay safe, find food and get mates. Swimming together, they look like one giant moving mirror. This is a great trick for startling and confusing predators.

In sparkly gowns, these fish unite
so hungry sharks won't take a bite!

Dazzling coral forests make perfect hiding places for equally colorful reef fish. Hungry sea creatures have a hard time seeing them.

To camouflage, bright reef fish hide
in fancy swimsuits as they glide.

Giant clams in frilly dress
make energy with great success.

A giant clam has its own solar energy
system. Shiny cells on its mantle reflect
sunlight inward. The algae living inside
its shell use that light for photosynthesis.
They share that energy with the clam.

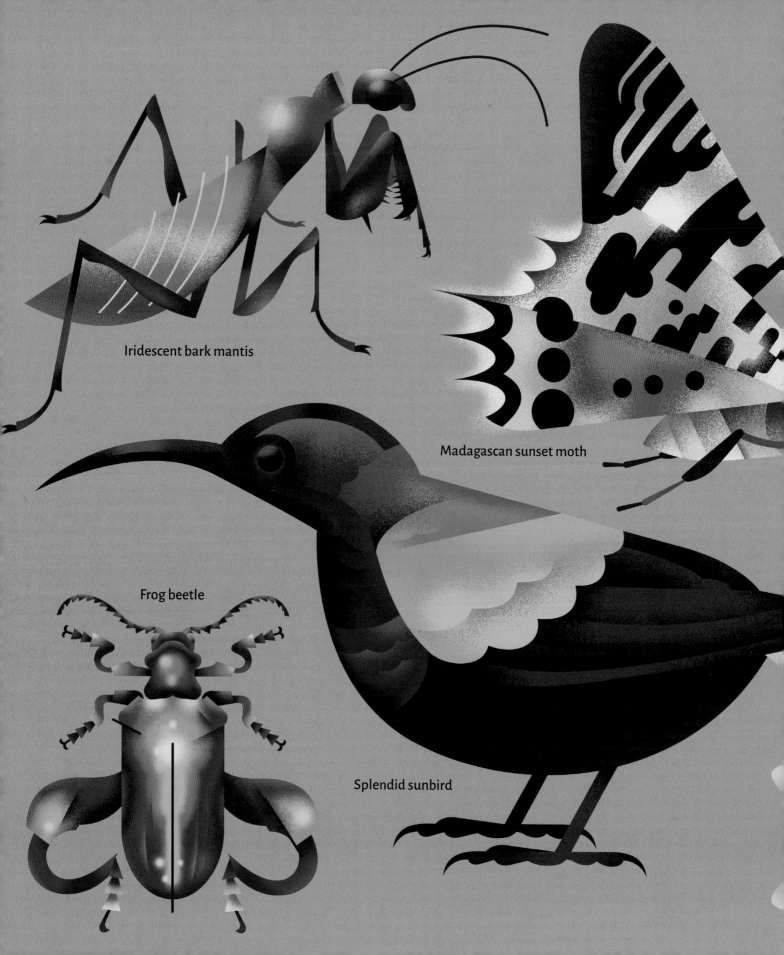

Iridescent bark mantis

Madagascan sunset moth

Frog beetle

Splendid sunbird

Sunbeam snake

On scales or feathers, shells or skin,
their sparkles stand out or blend in.
These adaptations pass the test
for animals who dress their best!

Blowfly

Siamese fighting fish

Shining a Light on Iridescence

Iridescence is nature's color magic! Blink and you might miss it.

Pretend you're looking at a peacock in the daylight. As you move — or he does — the colors of his feathers seem to change, too. They burst out, becoming brighter and more rainbow-like. This effect can happen quick as a flash, then disappear in a wink.

How does this happen? If you look at them through a microscope, some bird feathers, insect wings, shells, scales and animal skins have a special structure or layers to them. These structures bend light in different directions, "crashing" light reflections into each other. The "crash" creates a kaleidoscope of dazzling colors. That's iridescence.

Iridescent colors are an important animal adaptation. Animal adaptations are specially developed skills, behaviors or body parts that help animals to survive in their habitats. Iridescent animals wear bright, glittery colors to either blend in, like rainbow boas on the jungle floor, or stand out, like peacocks trying to catch the attention of peahens. Their sparkles help them escape predators, find mates, make energy, claim territory, survive temperature changes, camouflage, defend themselves, communicate, signal directions and more.

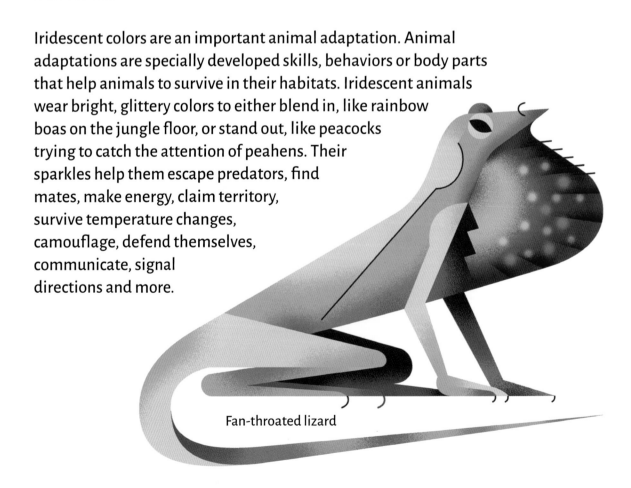

Fan-throated lizard

Caihong juji

Animals have been using iridescence since the dinosaur age. A recent discovery in China unearthed Caihong juji, a duck-sized dinosaur with iridescent feathers who lived about 161 million years ago.

Scientists are taking lessons from iridescent animals. For example, by studying beetles, butterflies, squid and other "camouflage experts" of the natural world, we can learn their tricks and apply them to human problem solving. Scientists hope to use their findings to develop new technologies. Camouflage materials, paints, cosmetics, medical devices and consumer electronics, are just a few of the possibilities. Maybe someday we'll invent materials or wearable devices that change colors in an instant. What a perfect way to hide in plain sight!

To my husband, John, for his steadfast love and encouragement on this writing journey and in life — KJ

To my buddy, Coco — DM

Sources

Doucet, Stéphanie M. and Melissa G. Meadows. "Iridescence: a functional perspective." *Interface Focus*, vol. 6, no. 2, 23 Feb. 2009. Online.

Eckstut, Arielle and Joann Eckstut. *The Secret Language of Color: Science, Nature, History, Culture, Beauty of Red, Orange, Yellow, Green, Blue, & Violet.* New York: Black Dog & Leventhal Publishers, Inc., 2013.

Honovich, Nancy and Darlyne Murawski. *Ultimate Bugopedia: The Most Complete Bug Reference Ever.* Washington, DC: National Geographic Kids, 2013.

Jenkins, Steve. *Living Color.* Boston: HMH Books for Young Readers, 2007.

Khan, Amina. "Scientists see evidence of iridescent rainbow feathers on a dinosaur." *Los Angeles Times*, 17 Jan. 2018. Online.

Read, Tracy C. *Exploring the World of Hummingbirds.* Richmond Hill: Firefly Books, Ltd. 2017.

Spelman, Dr. Lucy. *National Geographic Animal Encyclopedia: 2,500 Animals with Photos, Maps, and More!* , Washington DC: National Geographic Kids, 2012.

Text copyright © 2022 by Karen Jameson
Illustrations copyright © 2022 by Dave Murray

Published in 2022 by Groundwood Books / House of Anansi Press
groundwoodbooks.com

Groundwood Books respectfully acknowledges that the land on which we operate is the Traditional Territory of many Nations, including the Anishinabeg, the Wendat and the Haudenosaunee. It is also the Treaty Lands of the Mississaugas of the Credit.

We gratefully acknowledge for their financial support of our publishing program the Canada Council for the Arts, the Ontario Arts Council and the Government of Canada.

Canada Council   Conseil des Arts
for the Arts   du Canada

ONTARIO ARTS COUNCIL
CONSEIL DES ARTS DE L'ONTARIO
an Ontario government agency
un organisme du gouvernement de l'Ontario

With the participation of the Government of Canada   Canadä
Avec la participation du gouvernement du Canada

Library and Archives Canada Cataloguing in Publication
Title: Time to shine : celebrating the world's iridescent animals / text by Karen Jameson ; pictures by Dave Murray.
Names: Jameson, Karen, author. | Murray, Dave (Illustrator), illustrator.
Identifiers: Canadiana (print) 20210234814 | Canadiana (ebook) 20210235020 | ISBN 9781773064628 (hardcover) | ISBN 9781773064635 (EPUB) | ISBN 9781773064642 (Kindle)
Subjects: LCSH: Animals—Color—Juvenile literature.
Classification: LCC QL767 .J36 2022 | DDC j591.472—dc23

Each illustration in this book started as a small pencil sketch, was built in Adobe Illustrator, and finished in Adobe Photoshop.
Edited by Karen Li
Designed by Michael Solomon
Printed and bound in China

FSC MIX
Paper from responsible sources
FSC® C144853
www.fsc.org

Cape starling
Title Page:
Ruby-tailed wasp